WHERE CURLEWS CALL

A celebration in verse of Yorkshire

written by

JOHN NURSEY

with illustrations by
the author

All profits from the sale of this book will be passed to the charity Special Needs and Play Provisions York (S.N.A.P.P.Y.) a charity that provides help and facilities for children with special needs in York

OTHER BOOKS BY JOHN NURSEY

'WEEK-END IN THE VLLAGE and other verse'

'RIGHT TO ROAM and other verse'

'SILENT MUSIC and other verse'

'TIME REMEMBERED' (Edited)

'A SONG OF SEPTEMBER and other verse'

Published by J.R.Nursey, Forge Cottage, Flaxton, York, YO60 7RW.

Printed and bound by York Publishing Services Ltd.
64 Hallfield Road, Layerthorpe, York, YO31 7ZQ
Tel: 01904 431213   www.yps-publishing.co.uk

ISBN 978 0 9535193 5 4

The cover photograph is of the North York Moors at Bransdale

CONTENTS

ILLUSTRATIONS

PREFACE

This collection of verse brings together many of the Yorkshire poems that were originally included in 'Week-end in the Village', 'Right to Roam', Silent Music', and 'A Song of September', to which have been added others written subsequently.

The book does not in any way set out to be a sort of guide book of Yorkshire. Its contents largely represent purely personal incidents and memories relating to the County, for which I have great affection. It is hoped that this love of Yorkshire and its people will strike a chord with the reader and that he will perhaps capture in the verse some of the spirit of what is one of England's most beautiful counties.

None of the verse pretends to be 'clever' in the fashionable sense of the word; indeed it is all written in traditional forms that rhyme and scan and are easily understood by the reader. Nowadays such poetry is generally regarded as being out of date, and poetry set in metre and rhyme is invariably scorned by modern academics. However, all the verse in this book was written simply for my own personal pleasure without regard to any such considerations

As with the verse a few of the sketches have also been reproduced from the earlier books. Some of the illustrations relate directly to individual poems but others are of varied Yorkshire subjects and are included purely in the hope that they will bring an added interest to the book.

Forge Cottage   *John Nursey*
Flaxton

True Happiness

The measure of true happiness
  Is when a man can say
'No place on Earth I'd rather be
  Than where I am this day'.

In morning sun when I stride out
  On Marrick Moor in spring,
See Swaledale lying far below,
  And hear the skylark sing;

Or in the woods where Arkle Beck
  Goes tumbling to the Swale,
When sunshine filters through the trees
  And springtime fills the dale;

Or down in Coverdale, when may
  Hangs white along the bough,
I know that nowhere would I be
  But where I am right now.

Old Stocks at Bainbridge, Wensleydale

The Richmond Drummer Boy

For near a mile the tunnel ran,
　So legend had set down,
Hard by the bustling River Swale
　From Easby to the town.

It was the route for Abbey men,
　By which escape was made
To safety in the Castle Keep,
　From warring Scottish raid.

Long lost the tunnel on the hill,
　Till in the Castle ground
In eighteen hundred, or about,
　An opening was found.

Not known its use, nor where it led
　Beyond the Great Court yard,
And curious were the fighting men
　Who formed the Castle Guard.

Too small the hole for adult frame,
  The soldiers did employ
To enter through the opened niche
  Their little Drummer Boy.

With drum and coat of green and red,
  The boy, of twelve or so,
Crawled through into the opened way
  And underground did go.

He walked with steady beating drum,
  The soldiers taking heed,
And following the sound below
  To see where it would lead.

By Frenchgate and the Market Place,
  And ancient Lombards Wynd;
Down by the church to Easby Lane,
  With Richmond left behind.

The boy with beating drum walked on,
  The soldiers overhead,
Through Easby Wood towards the place
  The ancient tunnel led.

Then, as the Abbey came in view
  Some half a mile before,
A sudden silence did ensue,
  The drum was heard no more.

The little Drummer Boy, they say,
  Was never seen again;
His story and the legend ends
  Halfway down Easby Lane.

Beneath great oaks and sycamores
  A stone now marks the spot,
And tells in crumbling weathered words
  How far the boy had got.

Two hundred years have now passed by,
  But still the people talk
Of Richmond's little Drummer Boy,
  And of his famous walk.

And some say, when the nights are still
  And you pass by that way,
With muffled sound from far below
  You hear a drummer play.

Richmond Castle

Lilla Cross, North York Moors

Ryedale

Though far from Ryedale's homely soil
  Where distant duties draw
My heart lies in the heather still,
  High up on Wheeldale Moor.

And O that I was striding now
  Across the moorland hills,
Or down on Farndale's winding paths
  Among the daffodils.

In Castle Howard gardens now,
  Along the great Lime Walk
The wood anemones will show
  A carpet white as chalk.

When London streets burn in the sun
  And stale's the air and dry
I wonder if the meadowsweet
  Is out along the Rye;

And if Dick Green has started yet
   On bringing in the hay;
And what the fatstock heifers made
   At Malton sales today.

When winter slush is all around
   And London glooms prevail
I wonder if the wolds are white
   With snow, at Thixendale;

And if the winter sun shines down
   On Rievaulx in the snow;
And if they sledge at Terrington,
   Where we boys used to go.

Ah Ryedale! With your lovely hills
   And crisp clear moorland air,
Oh how I hold you in my heart
   And wish that I was there.

Skelton Tower, North York Moors

The Professional Yorkshireman

I am a true-born Yorkshireman,
   I'm Barnsley born and bred
And always speak in Yorkshire tones
   So no-one is misled.

Our house was just two up, two down,
   In Lower Leadmill Street;
A tin bath by the fire each week,
   And black boots on our feet.

My dad worked down the local pit,
   His job since he was young,
And died when he was fifty three
   From coal dust on his lung.

Myself, I have done well in life,
   And made a bit of brass;
In fact you could say I am now
   Quite upper middle class.

We Tykes, we are a breed apart,
   From God's Own Country made.
We're blunt and straight, don't suffer fools,
   And call a spade a spade.

I always talk of Yorkshire life,
   The beer, the corner shops,
The cricket teams and Headingley,
   Brass bands and Barnsley chops.

Of course, I do not live there now,
  (Be honest, nor would you.)
Our home is down in Sunningdale
  And worth a bob or two.

My golfing pals are stockbrokers,
  Sometimes a TV star.
Though Yorkshire's praise I'll always sing
  I'll sing it from afar.

York City Walls

Yorkshire Brass

From far and near the Yorkshire Brass Bands come
To Hardraw Scar when summer's decked in green,
And strains of cornet, trombone, horn, and drum
Re-echo through the lonely wild ravine.

A hundred years the contests now have spanned,
And long for some the journeys they entail
To battle for 'Best March', 'Best Hymn', 'Best Band'.
While in the nearby *Dragon* flows the ale.

Ah, Yorkshire Brass – the music of the hills,
Of woods and dales and wolds and lowland plain;
And Yorkshire bands with many a name that thrills –
Black Dyke, Brighouse, Grimethorpe, and Carlton Main.

West Riding men with coal dust in their soul
Who labour half a mile below the ground;
Rough men who toil with muscles hard as coal,
And yet such music! How sublime the sound!

If far from home I hear a brass band play
I yearn for windswept Yorkshire moors and heath,
And see again a cloudless summer day
With brass band playing on the Green at Reeth.

Such music speaks of homely Yorkshire grit,
Of comradeship that other counties lack;
That speaks of tumbling stream, and mill and pit,
And Ilkley Moor – ah, how it draws me back.

The Mist on the Moor

A morning mist hung on the moor
When I set out today,
Up by the Chapel through the wood
Along the hillside way,
Where all was bleak and grey.

Now past a crumbling ruined barn
And bridge across the beck
Along the lonely moorland path
Through thickening mist I trek,
And frosts the ways bedeck.

Small scattered pools lie frozen hard
About the peaty ground,
While now and then a startled grouse
From in the heather round
Creates the only sound.

Here, where the mist encircles me,
I feel about me then
From near two hundred years ago
Come lingering again
The ghosts of mining men.

A watery sun breaks through the mist
High up by Moor House Gill,
Where solitude and silence hangs
Upon the winter hill,
And all the world is still.

And in that wild and silent place
I sense, as I stride there,
How distant and how trivial
As if by answered prayer
Grows all my worldly care.

The War Memorial

Who now remembers William Banks,
A Private in the 1st East Yorks?
James Chapman, Bernard Lodge, John Horn,
Of these men now who ever talks?

Just names among a fading list
Of men upon the church wall plaque –
A plaque for Great War Askrigg lads
Who went but never did come back.

Was William Banks a shepherd's lad
Who tended sheep on Wether Fell?
A carpenter? A grocer's boy?
What life was his now none can tell.

A boy of only nineteen years
A life cut down before it starts,
Then just a sideboard photograph
And parents with their grieving hearts.

To us these men are little more
Than lines of marching faces seen
In some old silent jerky film
Upon a television screen.

Do any now who pass that plaque
Reflect on these and ever pause
To read the names, and ponder on
So much life lost in futile cause?

We will remember, glibly said,
But few, I doubt, will linger there,
And likely 'tis, the men who died
Will neither feel aggrieved nor care.

South Transept Rievaulx Abbey

Rievaulx Abbey

The wooded hillside rises steep and high,
The valley floor below lies thick with snow
Where stands the ancient abbey by the Rye,
Its great walls gleaming in the sunlit glow.
What splendour in this silent winter scene!
A beauty greater even than in June
When all the dale is lush with summer's green.
Fine crafted stone from local quarries hewn
Shows clear in windows, columns, arches, piers;
And white-clad monks at vespers in the night
I seem to see across eight hundred years,
Their shadows flickering in each candle's light.
Naught now but roofless walls in winter snow
Yet what a magic here that thrills me so.

The Lead Miners

I climb the lonely hillside path;
  The way is steep and slow;
I pause for breath, and in the dale
  See Reeth lie far below.

Two hundred years ago and more
  How different this path then;
With steady streams of mining carts,
  And trudging mining men.

In winter's dark they climbed the hill
  Before the morning light;
Went underground; and then emerged
  To see the black of night.

Five hundred feet below the ground
  The lead mine had its hub;
Along the levels miners toiled,
  With pick and rail and tub.

By candlelight they spent their days,
  In space enough to squeeze
Through tunnels long and dark and damp;
  With worsening lung disease.

On many great cathedrals now
  The lead which does survive
Was won by these who rasped and coughed,
  And died at forty five.

They led a hard but homely life
  By hearth at eventide;
Their houses now are week-end homes,
  With four-wheel drives outside.

In brass bands at the Institute,
  Where practice nights were held,
They played at Muker, Reeth, and Thwaite,
  At Gunnerside, and Keld.

But economics closed the mines
  By eighteen eighty eight;
The mining men then had no choice
  But up and emigrate.

I rest close by a tall brick stack,
  Now silent, cold, and still;
Then see the sun break through the cloud,
  And shine on Calver Hill.

Across the moor from where I gaze,
  The grass-grown trackway cuts
To where the waste heaps from the mine
  Now mix with Shooting Butts.

A mining hamlet lies close by,
  But time has done its worst;
Three houses and some crumbling barns
  Are all that's left of Hurst.

The air is crisp and brightly clear,
  A plover calls nearby;
And gently rustles in the breeze
  The heather where I lie.

I count life's blessings that are mine,
  That these men never got;
And feel a great humility,
  At this lonely moorland spot.

*The backbone of a rugby union club is invariably
formed by the veterans, usually former first team
players, who continue to play on in the lower sides.
Such a team is the Beverley Bandits.*

The Spirit of the Game

They play for honour of the club
   With pride in all their hearts
Fine men but – let's be honest here –
   A collection of old farts.

Deep down they know the skills they've got
   Are what the first team lack,
And if they only trained again
   They'd get their places back.

These days when they crash to the ground
   Far louder are the howls,
(They play on pitches grazed by cows
   That suffer from loose bowels.)

When fighting starts their language now
   Would shock a decent ref,
But now not only is he blind
   Thank God he's also deaf.

Then afterwards the Bandits show
   All's fair in love and war,
And with opponents in the bar
   Forget what went before.

The sod who punched them in the scrum
   No longer is a fool;
It's bonhomie and drinks all round,
   (Unless they're playing Goole).

Chapel-le-Dale, Ribblesdale

Those Who Died

Around the church the trees stand bare
Against the winter sky,
Below the lonely brooding moor,
With tumbling stream close by.
A haven from the icy chill
That grips the morning dale,
With Ingleborough and Whernside peaks
Enrapt in misty veil.

A little church of stolid build,
No idle pomp or fuss;
A stone flagged floor, a stone clad roof
On heavy timber truss.
The nave and chancel all in one,
Of simple form and line;
Scarce fifty feet, and much rebuilt
In eighteen sixty nine.

A Midland Railway tablet here
In memory of its dead,
Men killed while working on the line
From Settle to Dent Head.
Within the stillness of the church
I browse with idle thought
Through records of the railway years
And of the grief they brought.

Of men who laboured at Blea Moor,
Two miles or so from here;
A savage place, remote, and wild,
And windy, cold, and drear.
In shanty huts the families lived
Within that dismal scene,
At Inkerman, Sebastopol,
Dent Head, and Batty Green.

From brickworks' chimneys smoke and soot
Poured forth in acrid trail,
While blasting from the tunnel works
Re-echoed through the dale.
In mud and bog and boulder clay
Hard was the life men led;
And hard they toiled and hard they drank,
And hard the violence bred.

Men, women, children, – sad the tales
The sombre pages tell;
Two hundred souls lie buried here
From hutments in the Fell.
Huts rat infested, cramped, and foul,
With cesspits by the door;
No sanitation; squalid, and
Diseases by the score.

Of smallpox, cholera, I read,
And accidents to men;
So many deaths, and over half
Were children under ten.
Of blood, I read, crushed bones, and death
From wagons breaking loose,
Carts overturning, navvies killed
Through dynamite misuse.

I join again the Whernside scene,
A land of crags and caves,
Where snowdrops in the winter sun
Show white among the graves.
So peaceful now the churchyard lies;
'Tis hard to think such woe
And sadness did engulf this place
A hundred years ago.

So many graves and grassy mounds
Erected at this place;
Now disappeared, all levelled out
With no surviving trace.
The railway dead a churchyard plaque
Does solemnly recall,
To supplement the tablet stone
Upon the church west wall.

Yet up the dale at Ribblehead
A greater tribute stands –
The proud and massive viaduct
These built with their own hands.
Full square across the Pennine scene
This legacy survives
Of wives and children, and the men
Who toiled and lost their lives.

How few today, on railway jaunts
From Settle to Carlisle,
Would guess the cost in human life
Of every scenic mile;
Or as they pass by Ribblehead
Would ever understand
What hardship was endured by these
Here sleeping close at hand.

Ribblehead Viaduct, Ribblesdale

A moorland gate

The Wildlife Protectors

They fix a notice on the gates,
  Where moorland trackways go.
'Keep clear of nesting birds,' it states,
  'Respect for wildlife, show.'

They come again when Autumn bites;
  Their gundogs standing by
They line the birds up in their sights
  And blast them from the sky.

Arncliffe Bridge and Church, Littondale

Littondale

The church clock strikes in Arncliffe tower
Beneath an April sky;
The Skirfare on its pebbly bed
Goes murmuring quietly by.

Save for the water's rippling flow
All's silent, calm, and still,
And nothing stirs along the lane
That leads to Halton Gill.

I linger there among the graves
And springtime daffodils,
And feel the touch of Heavenly peace
Among these Pennine Hills.

All round me sleep old Arncliffe men
Who toiled for meagre wage;
And yet their headstones in the grass
Speak of a gentler age.

The old stone houses where they lived
For generations down
Are genteel now, and occupied
By strangers from the town.

By sycamores and village green
And past 'The Falcon's door
My way leads westwards up the hill
And on to Clowder Moor.

Along this path in years long gone
In sun and snow and gale
Walked monks and beasts and packhorse men
From here to Malhamdale.

Beyond the greystone village mill
Now steeply climbs the track;
Then high upon the hill I pause,
Stand idly looking back.

The valley floor lies far below
Criss-crossed by dry stone walls,
With old stone barns; and all that's heard
Are young lambs' plaintive calls.

The river winding through the fields
Where celandines abound
With lapwings wheeling overhead,
And Spring is all around.

At such a place, at such a time,
A sight I would not miss,
For never was there such a place
More beautiful than this.

Wharram Percy ruined church, Yorkshire Wolds

The Abandoned Village

The hillside path runs firm and dry
The morning air is frosty cold,
And blue's the early April sky
Above the rolling Yorkshire wold.

By Raisthorpe Wold and Deep Dale tops,
With stonework white in sunlit glow
Beyond a distant hawthorn copse
The ruins of St.Martin's show.

There Wharram Percy had its day;
Two manor houses, mills, and pond,
Eight hundred souls, whose houses lay
About this church and slope beyond.

But came the day the landlords found
That sheep and wool would better pay.
The farm men went; and all around
Was left abandoned to decay.

Five hundred years of sun and rain
Have worked their will upon this place
Till time has turned it green again
And of the homesteads left no trace.

No houses, streets, or village lanes,
All remnants gone of former days;
Naught but the ruined church remains
And hillside grass where cattle graze.

Below this lonely hillside sleep
Its dwellers of a thousand years,
Who lived and loved and earned their keep,
Knew joy and sadness, hopes and fears.

Now, solitary in the dale,
The church stands roofless to the sky,
Defenceless now to rain and gale,
A haunt of ghosts and night owls' cry.

Through window arch the early sun
Slants down upon the farther wall,
The only sound a millpond's run
And from the wold a curlew's call.

Richmond Falls

At Richmond Falls

The blood runs cheerless through my veins
   Here by the River Swale,
As waters from the springtime rains
   Come surging down the dale.

When I was young so many things
   We took for granted then,
That fashioned our awakenings
   As we grew up to men;

A pride in making England great;
   A steadfast C of E;
Fair play in games; great men of State;
   A loyal BBC.

But life today is not the same;
  Now everywhere we meet
Aggression; greed; someone to blame;
  And whingeing in defeat.

Where men of stature ruled the land
  Now little pygmies drool,
Dispensing England out of hand
  To European rule.

A populistic course they steer,
  No worth in what they say.
They tell you what you want to hear,
  Then act some other way.

They preach concern for others' plight,
  But privately agree
It's not a case of 'what is right',
  But 'what is right for me'.

The Church with trendyism creaks,
  Its faiths no longer stand.
The very language that it speaks
  Is juvenile and bland.

The BBC Correctness seeks;
  At England now it sneers.
Its tuneless pop forever shrieks;
  A torment to our ears.

As I stand here beside these Falls
  And watch the Swale plunge by
Somehow I sense to me it calls;
  Feels angry, just as I.

Yet as the foaming waters pour
  Towards the distant sea
Do they perhaps, within that roar,
  Say other things to me?

'You're getting old, you've had your day,
  No room for men like you,
Who cling to some out-moded way
  And can't accept what's new'.

In sombre mood I turn again
  From that wild thunderous roar.
Then as I climb the winding lane
  My spirits rise once more.

Above me by the castle wall
  The rooks are building now.
In sycamores they swoop and call,
  With cheerful raucous row.

The primroses are coming out,
  With blackthorn, on the hill.
Such life and beauty all about!
  There's joy in living, still.

A Man of Good Fortune

What fortune's mine, that I can stride
   For twenty miles and more
Across these wild and lovely hills,
   The heath stretched out before.

What joy to me, each time my path
   Across the moor I trace;
The springy turf; the curlew's call;
   The west wind in my face.

I think of other men, who trudge
   On hills beyond the sea,
With all their worldly goods on carts,
   In flight from tyranny.

And always do I wonder why
   A wretched man like me
Should be so blest in life and limb,
   And striding out so free.

Penyghent, Ribblesdale

The west pier Whitby

On Whitby Pier

Do you remember Whitby pier
When we two sauntered there together,
White horses breaking far and near
In wild and windy winter weather?

Waves beating on the outer wall
With foaming spray tossed to the sky,
Engulfing us in salty squall,
And overhead the seagulls' cry.

Exhilaration all around,
And we were young and fancy free,
Uplifted by the thunderous sound
Of that wild and boisterous sea.

The east cliff rising steep and high
Where red roofs climb and lean and lurch,
And on its crest against the sky
Wind howling round the ancient church.

Boats swaying at the harbour quay
Their tall masts bowing straight and stiff,
And on the beach the raging sea
Hard pounding at the western cliff.

Your sheepskin coat drawn close about
Against the biting winter air,
And hand in hand, with little doubt
We were the happiest strollers there.

Then homeward up by Skinner Street
With tea at Bothams on the way.
Where toast and fresh cream cakes we'd eat;
Ah, happy days for us were they.

I went down to the pier today
A wild sea raging just as then;
But now it all seemed bleak and grey
And how I yearned for you again.

And Bothams too is much the same,
White tablecloths and smartly run;
But absent, you; and when tea came
It was an order just for one.

Stile on Ilkley Moor

'Late of Cordilleras'

Beside the beck and ancient bridge
With ivy covered piers,
This church has stood, or part of it,
For near a thousand years.
When I come walking down the dale
The beckside path I trace,
And always am I strangely drawn
Towards this Holy place.
I climb the steep and narrow steps
Up from the hillside lane,
All lichen green with slippery tread,
And then the churchyard gain.
On through bold clumps of daffodils
The gravelled pathways lead
Towards the porch, near where I sit
And always one stone read.

With wife and child, James Allison,
Fifty nine, and 'Late
Of Cordilleras', so it says,
Died eighteen forty eight.
For long I wondered every time
Those words I read again.
An English man from Spanish soil?
Then some book did explain.
It was a farm two miles away
They'd wrested from the moors,
And named in time and memory of
Napoleonic wars.
Here's winter jasmine on the walls;
A bellcote with two bells;
A sundial, weathered, so that time
It now just vaguely tells.

A modern builder's had a go
But not much skill has shown;
The north wall's rendered with cement
Marked out to look like stone.
Within the porch the distant sound
Of chattering rooks I catch,
As I draw near the great oak door
With sliding plated latch.

Inside, all newly painted walls;
A roof now underdrawn;
High backed box-pews; an old stone floor
Uneven now and worn.
A vase of Easter lilies set
Close by the altar rail
Pours fragrance through the chancel arch,
And silence does prevail.
The air is cool and strangely still
Where ancient feet once trod,
And somehow deep within I feel
The still, small voice of God.
Here, open at the Easter words,
The lectern bible lies;
Luke's gospel, chapter twenty four.
The well-loved phrases rise
From off the slightly yellowed page
To tell the Easter news,
As here I stand and idly read,
As if to empty pews.
Above me on the chancel wall
A squire of long ago
Looks down from his white marble bust
On all who kneel below.
High Sheriff and a liberal,
The tablet does record
The church in eighteen thirty he
Extensively restored.

Here, Great War local volunteers
Are named upon a plaque;
This little hamlet eighteen sent,
And three did not come back.

The notice board close by the door
Contains a pilgrim's prayer;
A letter from the Diocese
About the Parish Share;
And underneath, a written note
With patterned edge surrounds,
Which says the Whist Drive in the hall
Has raised two hundred pounds.
Outside, the sun shines on the graves
And on the distant hills.
He, late of Cordilleras, sleeps
Below the daffodils.

The churchyard steps

At the Cricket

A day at the cricket at Scarborough
And Yorkshire are one wicket down.
Behind me a man on his mobile
Is ringing his wife back in town.

What news on the cooker, he wonders?
Is the man from the Gas Board there yet?
We gather he is and the problem is fixed;
Some blockage, it seems, in a jet.

A half an hour on and he rings her again;
She's just made the Fitter some tea.
They're having a chat and he's learning about
Their holiday down in Torquay.

The next call we learn that the Fitter
Is viewing their old photographs;
They're in the front room on the sofa
And joking and having some laughs.

The calls from the mobile continue,
(More frequently now, it appears),
And quieter become those around us
As we all sit there straining our ears.

He's ever so nice is the Fitter,
And we learn that his first name is Jim.
He's tall and he's dark and he's handsome,
And she's having a good laugh with him.

Now Yorkshire are making good progress,
And runs are quite easy to find.
But better by far than the cricket
Is the story unfolding behind.

Then we learn they are up in the bedroom.
She's taken him there, so it seems,
To show him the curtains she purchased
Last week down at Nicholls & Breams.

The next time he rings there's no answer,
And Yorkshire are now ninety eight.
Then when we look up, there we see him;
He's hurrying out of the gate.

Langthwaite, Arkengarthdale

Reeth Green, Swaledale

The Return Visit

We lay and talked all through the night
Till dawn began to show;
We saw then, in the morning light,
The dale all white with snow.
The homely Inn; the winter scene;
The joy that we did share;
I wondered if there'd ever been
A happier loving pair.

Again the Inn; again that sight;
Though youth and years have flown.
Again I've had a sleepless night;
But this time on my own.
Long gone the girl whose love I had,
And empty is my heart.
I wonder if the roads are bad,
And if my car will start.

The Old Town Bridge, Richmond

A Prospect of Richmond

Is there a more majestic sight
Than Richmond from the west?
The loveliest of English towns,
And this view is the best.

From out along the wooded dale,
And by the river shore;
Where down this swirling northern stream
The peat brown waters pour.

Where boulders at the water's edge
Form rivulet and pond;
And there ahead, the Old Town Bridge,
With Richmond Hill beyond.

The castle high upon the crag,
And outlined to the sky;
While near a hundred feet below
The Swale goes tumbling by.

I love the way old cobbled streets
And alleys climb the scar;
Up Bargate, Bridge Street, Chapel Wynd,
And on through Cornforth Bar.

Up to the cobbled Market Square,
The heart of this old town,
With obelisk, and old church clock,
And castle looking down.

And Newbiggin – its Georgian fronts
This street the finest make –
Tree lined and broad, a market once,
Where men burned at the stake.

Old weathered houses, tier on tier,
Rise to the alleys trail;
All built of local quarried stone,
And cobbles from the Swale.

But when I see it from the south,
From high on Sleegill Bank,
I think again, and wonder if
This view should higher rank.

Across the gorge the castle walls
Stretch proud across the hill;
In biting Pennine wind and sun
They speak defiance still.

Small wonder no marauding foe,
Or king in times long gone,
Did ever once attack this place,
Or take its ramparts on.

Part hidden now by sycamores
Close by the eastern walls,
Runs Millgate, winding steeply down
Towards the Richmond Falls.

And on a hill out to the west
Stands tall Culloden Tower;
A folly built to celebrate
The victory of the hour.

But then where Easby Lane climbs high
My doubts are more increased,
As I look out across the woods,
See Richmond from the east.

St. Mary's; Holy Trinity;
The Castle Keep behind;
Grey Friars' ancient oblong tower,
And Frenchgate; Lombards Wynd.

Ah Frenchgate! Lovely cobbled street
Where time itself stands still;
And in the eighteenth century lived
The Lass of Richmond Hill.

A watercolour Turner did
From near to this same spot.
Perhaps he did consider this
The best view of the lot.

But east and west and north and south,
All aspects please the eye,
As homes and walls and towers rise
Against the Yorkshire sky.

The Lifeboat Station, Flamborough, East Yorkshire

The Flamborough Lifeboat

When you walk by the shore along Flamborough Head
Where the great cliffs rise to the Yorkshire sky
Remember the men, as you leisurely tread,
The men of the lifeboat in days gone by.

The men who rowed out into wild raging seas,
And answered the call without question or pause.
What courage was theirs! What brave men were these!
Just a wide open boat with ten men at the oars.

Remember the souls out at sea in distress,
In the shadow of death and a watery grave;
All resting their hopes on the skill and success
Of a small boat and crew who were fearless and brave.

For twenty nine years with twelve men and a cox
The Forester gallantly put out to sea
To vessels in trouble or grounded on rocks,
And the lives that she saved rose to seventy three.

Remember *St. Michael's* and *Gertrude* before,
And *Middlewood*, serving the longest of all,
In thirty two years bringing safely to shore
A hundred souls rescued from ships great and small.

Men's names linger on with awards that were won
For gallantry shown in the years long gone by;
Bill Parker, two Pockleys, Bob Long, and Bill Dunn,
Who now in the churchyard all peacefully lie.

Give thanks that there lived such fine seafaring men
Who'd risk their own lives unknown strangers to save.
I dream about these and of all they did then;
O God how I wish I was near half as brave.

Old cottages at Arncliffe, Littondale

An August Reverie

I came down from the moor today
To meadow, hedge, and lane, and stile,
And in the scene that round me lay
I idly stood and dreamed awhile.

A drowsy calm of afternoon;
A cloudless sky, and no sound heard;
The rambling hedge with brambles strewn;
And silent fields where nothing stirred.

I thought, while leaning on a fence,
This lovely sight confronting me,
When I stand here a twelvemonth hence
Once more as beautiful will be.

Though soon this summer scene will fade
The earth will stir and flower once more;
A thousand summers has it made
And each as lovely as before.

The bindweed in the hedge will show
Once more its trumpets white and gay,
And butterflies flit to and fro
Round meadowsweet along the way.

The seasons' pattern onward steers;
What difference then a twelvemonth on?
None, save of my remaining years
Another will have come and gone.

The seasons come, the seasons go,
Each showing as it did before;
Unendingly God makes it so;
While man decays and comes no more.

In fifty years, perhaps, will lean
Upon this fence some passer by,
Who'll gaze upon this self-same scene
And love its beauty just as I.

Castle Bolton, Wensleydale

At Middlesmoor

Across the dale from Lofthouse Moor
The old church clock rings out the hour,
As I pass through the great oak door
Below the square-cut limestone tower.

Ah! A wedding here has been;
With stocks, carnations, lilies, set
About the altar, nave, and screen,
Their perfume heavy, lingering yet.

As here I sit and muse alone
The only sound that reaches me
A blackbird with its fluted tone,
Poured forth from churchyard bush or tree.

Such joyous song, such mellow notes;
Most English, this, of any bird.
In to the church his clear song floats,
Of such a beauty rarely heard.

Among the flowers that round me lay
Some voice within me seems to stir,
And speaks of my own wedding day
And fond remembered thoughts of Her.

At such a place as this we wed,
Naught but the church itself is changed;
The same quiet holy scene, bespread
With flowers all lovingly arranged.

I see this wedding held here lately –
The morning suits, the photographs,
Reception somewhere down in Pateley,
With friends, relations, toasts and laughs.

And for this pair. what hopes and fears?
What lies ahead for them, I wonder?
Will love grow deeper through the years?
Or fade, and cast them both asunder?

I join the hillside track anew,
The little hamlet left behind;
My path I once again pursue
Refreshed in limb and soul and mind.

By moor and field and grey walled lane
Light-hearted, I, and free from care;
Yet in my thoughts all day remain
The bird, the flowers, and the unknown pair.

Derelict barn in Nidderdale

High Upon the Snow Clad Moor

High upon the snow clad moor
Crisp's the air and clear and bright,
Ivelet in the valley floor
Far below lies wrapped in white.

Nothing stirs in all the dale,
Save at one far distant spot
Smoke drifts up in rising trail
From a farmhouse chimney pot.

Glistening white the moor is spread
In the sunlit morning glow,
Silent, save for crunching tread
Of my footsteps in the snow.

By my path a dead sheep lies,
Far from flock and homely fold,
Stark and still with staring eyes,
Frozen hard but feels no cold.

Soon will be, while lying there,
Torn apart by fox and crow;
Soon will both those eyes that stare
Only empty sockets show.

Flown, its soul – to who knows where?
Left the body where it lay
Lifeless in the moorland air,
Food for fox and bird of prey.

When the summer breezes lull
Round this wild and lonely place
Scattered bones and empty skull
Will remain its only trace.

What a transitory thing
Is all life upon the earth!
Life to which we vainly cling,
Filling days to little worth.

Few the valued things I've done
Or will do before I die,
When my earthly course is run
And I too will rotting lie.

Brief is life, so I must go
Striding out and all cares ban,
See the beauty of the snow
On the moorlands while I can.

Malham, Malhamdale

Scorton Feast – The Cricket Day

Away to westward rise the Pennine Hills
Now standing clear against the August sky;
While down the lane beyond the village school
The River Swale goes tumbling briskly by.

Around the Green old houses, chapel, inns,
Gaze in upon the annual Feast-day stage,
Where sportsmen, children, actors, fairground folk,
Play out the ritual from a distant age.

Along the wicket now the roller toils,
Heaved up and down by lads in white and cream;
The Sunday match, with play to start at one
Against a local invitation team.

Outside *The Farmer's Arms* a lingering lunch
At tables loud with clattering plate and cup,
While from the Green there comes the mellow sound
Of bat on ball from players knocking up.

Mid afternoon and Scorton now are in,
The Policeman batting with the Policeman's son.
With lusty blows the fours come thick and fast
And twos and threes and singles nimbly run.

Spectators lounge behind the boundary rope;
The village Doctor, gammy leg and lame,
As umpire sits upon his shooting stick
And sees fair play is done throughout the game.

Outside *The Heifer* ribaldry abounds
Among the drinkers seated with their beers.
As time advances faster flows the ale,
And every six is struck to louder cheers.

Below the flowering cherry near the hall
The Reeth Brass Band in coats of emerald green
Plays well loved medleys, songs, and country airs,
And *Edelweiss* now floats across the scene.

The fielding side leap up in loud appeal
For any hopeful 'leg before' or snick,
But at the bowler's end the Doctor smiles
And merely readjusts his shooting stick.

The innings done the players all adjourn
Inside the hall for tea and homemade cake;
Then play resumes, the visitors to bat;
Two hundred runs and ten they need to make.

When stumps are drawn the ancient school tower clock
In evening sun shows twenty five to eight;
The players to *The Heifer* make their way,
Then loud the mirth and bedtime will be late.

The Yorkshireman and his Dog

He sups his pint of Theakston's ale,
Its froth all round his mouth,
And scorns the poncey incomers
Who've come here from down t'South.

Why can't they stay where they belong,
These ghastly southern hordes?
He only ever goes down there
When Yorkshire play at Lords.

He owns a Yorkshire terrier,
A yappy little beast;
You'd think he'd have a proper dog,
A Rottweiler at least.

But then you start to realise
When thinking through the thing
As Yorkshire's representative
This dog knows he's the king.

No need for him to grow long legs
Or muscles firm and large
All other dogs are well aware
Of just who is in charge.

Mere chicken bones wrapped up in hair
Yet fierce and unafraid;
And if this little chap could speak
He'd call a spade a spade.

He'll take on anything in sight
All beasts ten times his size,
And when he does it makes you wince
To hear their painful cries.

He may look nondescript to you
But don't suggest a fight
For as his teeth sink in your heels
You'll know he's got it right.

Richmond from the Green

Lines written when idling through a book of Frank Sutcliffe's photographs.

I idly turn in this old book
Each haunting sepia printed page,
And at another world I look
Of distant harsh but tranquil age.

These photographs of long ago,
All centred on this seaside place,
Reveal a life we'll never know
Contained within each captured face;

And somehow I am backwards drawn
In to that age, where every scene
Suggests to me some hardship borne
Or joys and fears there might have been.

Here ragged urchins play and laugh;
Here cart with horse that slowly plods;
Top hatted railway station staff;
Here chimney sweep with brush and rods.

Across the harbour in full sail
Here moves a pair of Whitby yawls;
Here women at the harbour rail;
Here ancient dames with crocheted shawls.

What scenes of drama are set here
That hauntingly these pages show,
Though crude the camera, plates, and gear
That captured them so long ago.

These fisher girls along the Quay –
Did they perhaps keep watch and pray
On nights when wildly raged the sea
For loved ones' safe return next day?

These boys around a boat at play
In eighteen eighty six; what then
The fate of all these lads, when they
Had grown to working Whitby men?

This lifeboatman what tales might tell
Of shipwrecks, gallant deeds he knew;
Who, when one tragedy befell,
Was sole survivor of his crew.

Hard was their life and never free,
Yet still within each homely face
That from the page looks out to me
A quiet contentment there I trace.

A hundred years have now gone by,
And lanes and yards and homes and Quay
Now modern faces occupy;
But few show joy it seems to me.

Now we are free, no more the threat
Of workhouse, poverty, or pain,
And comfortable our life; and yet
Man's heart in joy shows little gain.

Micklegate Bar, York